The Book of Jeweled Visions

for Martha

The Book of Jeweled Visions

how to do it

        anew

                each time

as is the case

        with the worlds

              the words

a most pleasant

Robert Schuler

colleague

Robert Schuler

March 18, 2010

MWPH BOOKS

Fairwater, Wisconsin

Many of these poems appeared previously in the fol-
lowing journals: *Architrave*; *Baybury Review*;
Beauty/Truth; *Blueline*; *Brevities*; *Chiron Review*; *Coal
City Review*; *Ekphrasis*; *Farmlit*; *Foliage*; *Free Verse*;
Hummingbird; *Indefinite Space*; *Kaleidoscope*; *Lilliput
Review*; *Mid-America Review*; *Northeast*; *Pebble Lake
Review*; *Plainsong*; *Red Hawk Review*; *Saturday's Poem*;
State Street Poetry Sheet; and *Wavelength*.
   Mississippi Valley Review
I want to thank all of the editors of these publications
for their support, and I want to give special thanks to
the following editors for their encouragement of
those of us who are intrigued by small poems: John
Judson, *Northeast*; Phyllis Walsh, *Hummingbird*, and
the *Hummingbird* bookmark, *a tryptych for May*;
Linda Aschbrenner, *Free Verse*; Joyce Odam, *Brevities*;
and David Rogers, *Wavelength*.

MWPH Books
PO Box 8, Fairwater, WI 53931
ISBN 978-0-974 64-99-6-2

This book is dedicated to Carol,
my constant inspiration.

Dans nos ténèbres, il n'y a pas une place pour la Beauté.
~~Tout~~ la place est pour la Beauté.
Toute   René Char, *Feuillets d'Hypnos*

for van Gogh
        "I am in a continual fever of work."

what is art
the world rushing in
lemon-yellow
Prussian blue
rose-speckled black
the spawn   the spread
the unleashing
the more sketches   the more
articulations
of wind   flowers   trees
leaves
that which
makes
us   breathe
alive

about writing

there is no exit
there is no beginning
to mind or time
the wind or the world
lined with false passages
tricked with light
the bull disappears into stone

*

cancellation

Mr William Blake will not appear
today nor at any time in the future
he has no wish to please
or to proselytize
he would rather walk with the angels
given to the rivers and the woods

song

the artist must sing the truth
however oddly   as in
Green Dolphin Street
offered as a gift in Stockholm
almost holy
clean   pure
every note believed
crafted   a ringing jewel
and then Coltrane barrels
out *el toro negro y azul*
liquid lyrical melancholia
sweet love pouring out
into the Stockholm night
my night summer Wisconsin
past four in the morning
be-bopped   haunted
worried over   loved
revered   damn I love you so much
I don't care if I've missed a note   botched
a word or a step   I'm going to hold you
forever dance with you past death

for Howlin' Wolf

we keep talking
about
the real world
what a howler
god bless you
how can I send
the truth
raw
        back to you

*

mornings my lover
rescues palominos
pale   like doves
owls   and hawks
all of the majestic
animals abandoned on earth

August sunset

glassy rain
orange-red moon
steams down
past black Chinese pines

*

descargas

let's make the moment
mambo blue
why hold back our loves
ringed by the drums
tenors roaring through the night
flutes swirling
sweet through the trees
the long grasses broken
under the heavy rush of trumpets

fiesta picante

the poem is
what's alive
the blessing come
into the mind
bluebirds sailing
past black fences
the scalding saxophones
of Tito Puente's mambos

*

for Stevie Ray Vaughan

"I'm cryin'   Why do I
have to feel this way"
how many lovers have fallen
behind in the dust
where are we all running

5:30 PM, Saturday, November

wide beams of light
fall   misty
gold through the black
cathedrals of branches

*

walk the sandpaths
between the pines
write poems to rhythms
you've never heard before

*

long after midnight
the soul wanders
the deserts of the long streets
with the poor   the lost
the lovers   the aimless wind

"el olor de cuerpo"
                Cortázar

your skin is jasmine
lavender   rosemary
spiced with basil
the hazy smoke of sage
the scent of stars
fallen
          scorching sand

*

early January sunset

on the ridges of the valley
black branches fan
out into the rose-
lavender haze
sickle moon cut
into the marbled
blue-black night

jazz

the summers of Illinois
the sweating sheets
what are you doing here
fumbling with these beauties
these treasures
where do the rains come from
the flowers
Stan Getz
some secret well
of melancholy beauty
early autumn
fluting
blue man

*

I do not believe
we will ever die
the winds singing
rain in the pines

notes on Carl Dreyer's *La Passion de Jeanne d'Arc,*
1928

where is the scribe
        the penman
        the witness
the Grand Inquisitor   strolling   does not see
the long shadow of the cross
spread across Jeanne's cell   the bleached white
bones of walls
his boots crush the ashes
the fasces of wood and wheat and weeds
the skulls of saints
the detritus   the waste that is history
we keep making

traveling through the night
after Howlin' Wolf's "Smokestack Lightning"

I'm still chasing your train
"shinin just like gold"
hollering out after you
like a wolf to the moon
I've been loving you
since first light
never gonna hold you
tight enough
never gonna sleep

*

walking deep into winter

it is a blessing to walk freely
what are the names of the small birds
the ones with blue wings that sang
at noon in the Colorado blue spruce
what are the names of the stars falling
through the mazes of the oak branches

"Who's been talking?"
        Howlin' Wolf

that long winter he learned
to listen to the wind again
to dream of all the women
who danced in the wind
the rhythms of the patterns
of the shadows over the snow
the blue words of the wind

*

Illinois twilight, December

dusky leafsmoke
flooding west
broken open
by molten golden
and wine-red
sunfall

after Vallejo

the long afternoons are bitter
with shadows and prayers
I have forgotten
we must walk down
halls and valleys
in which the wind smells of must
and sand and death
I wish for rain
       and the blossoming of owls

*

Cinco de Mayo

cardinal dancing
a prince   a lord
down the green
mazes of the osiers

at St. Jean de Luz, after Vallejo

sand blown down
the moon broken
riding the waves
in the distance
the mist leaves
white jewels

*

in the slant
of late fall light
still on an elm's limb
two blue owls

bluesman

R.L. Burnside
Independence, MO
knew a little more
than most of us
about putting it
down on the line

*

secession of one

some say
you just can't write
that way
what matters is that I can
say what I have to say
about
this farce we live
on Eden-earth

July 23rd   stormset at noon

the western sky   black   aboil
swirling wild with charcoal shreds and chunks
green-tinged at the top
the rain seething gray
through the trees
bent to the ground

*

listening to *Générique* by Miles Davis

the runs of the springing horns
past the drums and the bass
why have I lived
this life trapped
in the mind   in the body

what is it
what goes on outside
this ghost of self

*

Listening to Miles Davis' *"I Thought about You"*

there was nothing
much else to do
I'm hung in the wind
lost in space
stuttered words
bottoming out
echoing down
canyons

*

rain falling
in cups of leaves
for the sparrows

after Reverdy

the admiral butterfly
orange-winged
still on the bindweed
crows squawking in the shadows
a cardinal pitched like a curve
through the shadows
breezes nudging the daylilies
a grapevine dangling down
awaiting an arbor
blue streams overhead
we have not seen our knight
the hawk
as we listen to Scriabin's piano sonatas
bee-balm
blue cornflowers
golden coreopsis
a few pale red poppies
the black woods always burning
gold in the west   flickering
I have no idea
why we are alive

Legends

According to Herodotus, in Babylon every woman must, at least once, visit the temple of Aphrodite, where she can find a man she wants and tempt him to have sex with her outside the sanctuary. I dream you have chosen me.

this is
the real thing
when we go
down to the ground
the dusty grass
the haymound
rolling our asses in the mud
bones and skin lost in the mist
the straw-must
the nasty shrieking crows
this is the royal way
El Camino Real

*

caught in the copper
wires of the willows
plum moon

walk for years
shoeless
past Horse Thief Coulee and Gypsy Ridge
to the river's source
the ocean   the shrines of the saints
where the owls and eagles tell us
of the daily betrayals
of our souls

*

res publica

the worst of us is
our tepid indifference
"who gives a shit"
Jesus spits us out
we're dying inside
all along the line

the structure of Schubert's "Death and the Maiden"
the swiftness of the deer
the scintillating beauty of the silver razors of death

*

backwaters, winter light, Alma, Wisconsin

swans floating
down the black
cracks of the channels
forever over
silver pools
under the long black bluffs
stained wine-red at sunset

*

spring thaw

two eagles stand in the dark center of the lake
broken platelets of ice whispering   rasping
shuddering under the rough gusts of blue wind

winterfall

walking stormwind
thudding bones
through the old prairie
threaded with deerpaths
hollowed into bowers
winding out   towards the lake
strands of big bluestem   mullein
Indian grass   blasted down
whistling   white-capped
waves rolling in   wobbling with woodducks
bluebills and goldeneyes

*

Poem for the New Year

a year spun around again
and what have I done
what is to be
                done

spring, for the buzzards

spicing the loose
hairy gray clouds
three zopilotes float
circling
      one
          another
riding the spring winds
moving inland from the Mississippi
reinhabiting
gracing the green strings of the summer valleys

*

the art of poetry

watching the dance-
steps and the slow
looping flights of egrets
snow geese and white pelicans
while listening to Stan Getz play
Live in Paris

Ikon at twilight

two eagles pause
on a broad blue elm
in the gauzy rose air

*

to make
beauty
solid
in a broken world

*

all the people I meet
know the ropes
in which
they are hanging

to stand here
in the midst of the woods
shadows shot with light
falling and fallen
leaves   scarlet-browned
pale yellow   apricot   gold
in love
lost amidst
what's left
sing for it   now

*

"a door to glory"
        Joyce Cary

went down the wrong
road   lucky
not all the way   ·
swerved
off into the darkness
doorways cracked with light

report from the interior, February 24th

driving home through horizontal snowfalls
runnels of salt and sand
staining the windows
an absence of hawks
no music worth a damn
for days   past the voices of brimstone
and fire
and the false
boundaries of states

*

Easter, again

snow spins
down
over the sun-
yellow tulips
thick through smoke   wet oak
logs sputtering sparks
Donald Byrd's trumpet rising crystal
"Cristo Redentor"

31

listening to Chopin

passing the hours
with *valses*   *études*
dreaming in the rain

or the four *scherzi*
dreaming of hawks
dancing in the rain

*

history:
the Levellers were always right
it is never the just
but just the rich
who run the show

June 1st

midnight   seated at my desk   as usual
I am surrounded   comforted
by books   worn   shoved into
shelved
into their homely wooden stalls
that ladder up the walls
and I am as usual restless
want to run andante
with six flute quartets of Handel
out into the hazy warm summer night
through the lavender irises
rising high
past
unjust wars
the sufferings of the poor
all of the lost souls
towards the possibility of mercy

the structure of Sonny Rollins' "The Bridge"
his solos
fierce
lost
halting
pouncing
percussive
iron webs spun above
the drums of Elvin Jones
making
a bridge
crossing from madness into art

*

Winter seclusion

all night rains rattle and howl
with the wind
along the sere black bluffs of the Mississippi
entering the realms of silence and ice

the American Millennium

my old man said he could buy
whatever he wanted
I'm just looking around
to see what's left

*

August

cardinals dart
round the white
fluted blossoms
of the hedge bindweed
vines rising out of
steaming gray-green shadows

skiing in the rain

skis whispering
crackling across icy snow
past a flock of strutting ring-necked pheasants
white
mist roaring and whirling out of the black
alley of oaks

*

just before sunset, Baraboo, Wisconsin

summer heat sinking
smoky gray
under the high leggy white florets of yarrow
the lavender spikes of bergamot   gaudy
orange Turk's Caps
nestling in the notched shadows of the western
          hills

late July, Devil's Lake

at noon a dozen turkey vultures
ride the ridges
circling one another   spiraling upwards
dancing down air
just above the tumbled
lavender   pink   and dark purple stones
and the pines that spring
miraculously from them

*

summer cresting

at twilight the yellowjackets sail
home and nest in the west garden
the gathering
angry thunder
deep under the swaying
golden-brown daylilies

quid ultra

what do I do
can I do   each day
that might be sacred
holy   admire the flowers
and birds   pageants
of color and grace
cleanse with water
                    and reason
read and meditate

*

riffs

what will you do
when the rhythm section
calls you back
to reality?

history:
have you seen
the dazed slaves of the marketplace

*

flocks of goldfinches bouncing
feeding on the dusky seedhusks
of woodland sunflowers   stalks
swaying in slow summer wind

*

late fall

snow-crusted branches
collapsing
the hummingbird spins
away
in the rain-wind

The Last Judgement
scene from Andrei Tarkovsky's *Andrei Rublev*

the blank white
walls of the cathedral
it is false
it is impossible
to paint God
as Stalin
as Terror

*

alla prima, **return of the hawks**

on the highway to Madison
lilac and dark purple and black
clouds wheeling
past the car windows at sunset
and hawks   heads lifted high
white and cinnamon breasted
bursting
out of the misted thickets

Monet's "Poppy Field in a Hollow near Giverny"

we stand in the middle of a bowl
patched with washes of light red sand
loose tan scree   runs of blue-green
and high blue-white grasses
tinged with mauve
edged above with wind-
blown dark-green shrubs
overhead clouds foam
the poppies stretch a rich orange-red carpet
unrolling beneath our feet

*

poem

to sing
for no reason
or for many
thousands of reasons

for Art Blakey and the Jazz Messengers

hard April rain
thunder rumbling in the background
bebop
these drums gonna
shatter the walls
shock and shiver the mountains
down
these long droning
rams' horns are the horns
of processions and celebrations
wild and unchristened
Dionysiac   mystical

*

Albion Rose, for Blake
after Blake's *The Song of Los*,
Color printed from a copperplate

in wonder child Los watches
the sun rise rose-red
out of the black lake of chaos

a dozen eagles
perched
stocky black
in one white elm
under snowy bluffs
charcoalled with oaks

*

Indiana Morning

lay these strokes down
thick
across the gray canvas
hawks hanging
against the hard winds
near Eagle Creek
Monk and Coltrane riding high
out of Carnegie Hall 1957
past the blaze-red bushes

November

all of the willows in Illinois
along the roads
tossing
their long yellow-green braids
back
and
forth
in the hard winds

*

I think the meaning of poems
is to keep creating them

*

writing
       out of chaos
       out of love
       against time

Charlie Parker's *Red Cross*

be-
bop
seems to be
spontaneous wildness
but is in-deed
the intricate harmonic
choruses of monks
driven to jazz
cloistered in jazz
high-
way beyond boo and snort and booze
and the chaos of race

*

sing
along the edges of the mountains
the kingdoms

this morning   mad
with winds   cold   north
splintering   shivering   shattering
heaps of leaves
toppling the matchsticks of fences
scouring dust
off the streets
and the faded red bricks
the skeletons of the city
the roar in the mind
the scraping away
to the clean sanity of things
blow the man down

*

bless the hills
to stand in the wind
to watch the hawks
to feel this grace
rising

January 21st
"Mysterious Traveller"

herds of bison graze
heads down
round snowy meadows
wild turkeys peck in cornfield stubble
overhead an eagle saunters
wild geese loop in the milky blue west
deer pause at the edge of the woods
as we pass by   children of fortune
exulting
within Weather Report's "Nubian Sundance"

*

April Diary

round the tiny pine tree
in the middle of the woods
flocks of bloodroot
sheer white
blossoms shimmering
out of the dust of last year's leaves

driving in Peru today

the Town of Peru
past the modest graves
Cranberry Creek   Dushan Creek
Fall Creek   Meridean Slough
Rocky Creek   Rock Falls
the meandering ice-shelved blue Chippewa River
under the hawks   floating in the cold wind
the fresh blue air   spiced with salt
some of us have got
our wits about us

*

February 4th, afternoon

so much color in a winter afternoon
the blue wrinkles of Little Bear Creek
pastel blue sky stretching out beyond
cardinals in shellacked black woods
rose haze rising on the western hills

still-life

in the black wire basket
on top of the refrigerator
globes of brown-skinned
onions and potatoes
the white
ghost   the homunculus
garlic
hiding on the bottom

*

late May on the Mississippi

shadows of the wings
of vultures shuddering
over a field sewn thick
with incandescent
magenta phlox

it is a war
between sorrow
and love

*

blue lumière

to write
to praise
is to exist

*

art:
Egon Schiele paints the raw
wounds
flesh was born for

Prothonotary warbler

hooded bright golden-yellow
like a medieval Catholic scribe
shining in the still water below
swamp-singer sings
       zweet-zweet-zweet-zweet
          zweet-zweet
ringing off the flooded hardwoods
hackberry   sweetgum   the elms

*

walking meditation

the old railroad bed
cut out of the hills
rising along the river
thousands of chattering
Bohemian waxwings
joyous
banqueting
gorging on the rich spill of seeds

farm near Black River, early March

blue ice shines
in the boxed cranberry bogs
hawks sail
low
down the rising spring meadow
past
the boards of the barn weathered silver

*

listening to Shostakovich   II

the painful stretching of the violin
and cello strings
the suffering of the Jews
on the cross
why
stop crying
over all of the stones
there is no end
to our evil

why live lives imprisoned
in society and lies

*

Van Gogh
saw *la gloire*
of it all

*

March 23, after a letter of Van Gogh

Sunday you would have seen a vineyard
red as poured Cabernet   the distance spun
into yellow   and then a spring grass-green
after the rain the earth turned
violet here and there   glistening gold

April 1

a hawk's white
striped-faint gray
underbelly and wings
spread out
still
floating the spring thermals
riding
over the roads
the woods   the new houses
invading her ridges

*

what is the soul's weight in the wind

*

Rouault
a raw Christ
of art

April 7th

a misty distillation
a gathering
together
of
hammering woodpeckers
sawdust spilling out of black
trees
into pools of rain
a blue wash over all

*

April 30th

in the spring-sodden ditch
swarms of gnats
clumps of swamp cabbage
the jewels of the marsh
marigold

American history VI:
my funny valentine
didn't fit
Miles didn't fit
Desmond didn't fit
surrounded by all of this
supermarket music
drowning
in Madison's "commercial republic"

*

in the garden

waiting
wanting
to find which of you
are wild
flowers
which of you
weeds

from the Spanish

this morning is
light tingling
with music   we're trying to sing

*

when the sun breaks
through the dogwoods
the music runs beyond
we are abandoned here

*

religio

we have built
murderous
churches of blood

April noon, near Rice Lake

huge eagle busting up
out of the snow-blotched ditch
black wings tilting down
inches above the ground
floating sideways and low through
shadowing the papery birch copse

*

**Robert Bresson's *Diary
of a Country Priest***

the priest's soul painted
into the mesh of the film
out of a tenebrous mass
of trees   entangled
trunks   and branches
whispers of light rising
radiating   outwards

Improvisation

for my next painting
I will be the "knight who hath trespassed"
you the queen of the rose garden
who has cast me into a trance
and I will wander with you
down shadowy paths
terraced with blue roses
let us paint quickly   and richly
we are being swept away
into death

*

Monet's *Wheatstack, 1891*

in the background   red-gold
swirls of sun   diffused
a purplish conical mound
rises out of a farmfield flecked gold
stands in the middle
of lavender-stained waves of white mist

July 23, Sunday

the butterfly
a Tiger Swallowtail
pale yellow
with black stripes
scorched down her wings
nestles in between
the petals of all
the six-stalked
scarlet day-
lilies blossoming
in the garden

*

we have been told
we live small lives
while we are eating our dinner
into the feeder in the window
comes first the rose-breasted grosbeak
then the Ruby-throated hummingbird
burning rose out of her shining green wings

Jazz meditation, after Bonnard

bordered with books
this simple underground room
dissolves into the woods
seeded with wildflower gardens
lavender   blue   rose
in which Coltrane
slams the hammer down now
"Round Midnight"
cannonades of saxophones
blasting out
sheets of sound
bittersweet tenor runs
"vast emptiness   no holiness"
worlds of owls
Coltrane's long gyring
songs of love
"Ah-leu-cha"
the clashing brassy counterpoint
of trumpet and tenor
all is in the flourishes   Coltrane's
burnished riffs
grace notes
all is grace
burnished by sun

flowering in the garden
the blood's rhythms driven
by Philly Jo's drums
what hauls your through
the dull days   the sleepless nights
Pascal's dark terrifyingly empty places
become Bonnard's
skin-close intimate spaces
drenched   jeweled with light

I want
"All of You"
in the steaming bathroom
rose-pink
you are lovelier than a Bonnard nude
in her temple tiled blue gold and mauve
*"Et ces couleurs prènnent tout à coup une densité
tragique: il faut les saisir avant le fin."*

Miles Davis, *frelon brun*

bebopping it down
frelon brun
what's it all about
can we drum it up
sanctify the seconds
the woods   the hawks
the winds want to drum it up
the light falling
swirling
over the pools of the river
who is the drummer
I want to be
the hornet
who hammers the air
frelon brun
stinging your mind
getting the whole going

El Mambo Último

Tito Puente's "Jitterbug Waltz"
I'm rocking so high
I'm crying with joy
rhythms   congas   bongos
timbales   racketing   out
the night swelling
desire   into madness
I chase the laughter of the gypsy woman
from shadow to shadow
the drunken trumpet
shrill   strutting   torching the streets
vaulting over the storm clouds
the concertina trombone
a grumbling gypsy clown
this bright jouncy brassy
glassy ballroom
shattered
by the rasp and the roar
the guttural lust of the baritone sax

listening to mambos, floating out of May

the vision I have
of Eden   shines and glows
groves of silver blue flowers
and mad jazz saxophones
wandering and winding in between them
dances
          endless
                    dances of
blue and green
Matissean   men and women
chanting
choiring
this
blessed
instant

the baritone sax strikes like a snake
roars and whirls
sinuous   visceral

driving through the night

to beat a March snowstorm
from the top of Wisconsin   Cornucopia
to the middle   Menomonie
though Bayfield   Washburn   Cable
Hayward   Drummond   Ridgeland   Barron

you my love fall asleep and I wonder
why the lives lived in the towns we race by
are considered minor marginal meaningless much
less important than those lived
in London   Washington   Hollywood

unknown
who are we   what is our rank
so rich
with what we saw yesterday
the white breasts of the hawks perched
in the dark olive trees all along the road
the Namekagon shining through snow
huge tusks and mushrooms of ice sprouting
from the red caves carved out of Lake Superior's
          shores
the twisted cross and the white-laced green crown
of St. Mary's Orthodox Church in Cornucopia

offered by Russian lumbermen in thanksgiving
for the first harvest of berries and apples
evergreens rising high against the simple white
          planks
branches leaping up in the wind

*

She-hawk, March 13

I swear I saw her rise
in the midst of a blizzard
snow blown sideways
streaming over roads
car windows thudding
she-hawk riding up
breast and wings
blossoming into wind
in this raw whiteness
just outside
Champaign Illinois

August: walking the silence of Vimalakirti

the river of a day
wanders
past spent columns of sunflowers
sprays of goldenrod   asters smoking lavender
rabbits scatter   pheasants sputter
out of bleached underbrush   flickers whir-
scar blurred air
long heavy steps of self fall
silent into sand
how
does it hold
nothing is
here

*

early April

last year's long withered grasses
shawl the fallen
logs and vines lying
along the edges of the woods

paradeizo

the green roofed
summer pavilion
far across the Mississippi
at Lake Pepin   next to
the snow-dusted pines
adorned with hundreds
of the still   black
buddhas of eagles

*

Stop-time

steam-soaked August
green ridges recede
to gray   miles in the distance
egrets and herons prance
slowly in the shallows
eagles sail
until they dissolve
into veils of haze

Trempealeau Refuge, May

the great egret wades into the inlet
stands still as a statue   a slim white buddha
presides   hours over the wind-blown marsh
the lush marsh marigolds
the ferns unfurling from their fiddleheads
the herons who face east like bhikkus
the white pelicans prancing along the stony island
the white-rumped northern harrier patiently waiting
where the water just touches the leafless woods
crisscrossed
cristcrosse   with the golden-yellow heads
the yellow bodies and wings of warblers
the scarlet-red threads of tanagers
the drum and hammer of woodpeckers

*

three wrens looping
light round and round
shadows of the oaks

rain, late April

he swings the farmhouse door open   and watches
the rain fall   hard for hours
rill along the hillsides
well out of the hollows
sometimes you see single drops
diamond-shaped   spherical   spear-like
silvered   or blue   glistening
in the morning   the gray
woods will be mazed with green
bushes and reeds and grasses
the soil sodden black
the must-fresh birth-death smell of earth
and trees washed clean
a beginning   again
now the thud and puddling of windows
the walking rackets across the roof
and the skylight   crackling
lightning

Phoebis

perched on the edges
of the clearcut forest
her orange wings
soaked in blood

*

walking, late August

the trail is a world
of dust and haze
of drooping yellow coneflowers
high-rising daisies
darting monarchs
goldfinches and cardinals
and the sweet sweeps of sudden summer rain

the structure of the ruffed grouse in darkness
horned-feet snick-snicking over the leaves
wings drumming whirs
hard up the stony ravine

*

in the springs
of the feeder creek
skunk
bathing

*

February thaw

the smoky white and rose hills
the shimmering red-gold farmhouse
windows of winter

sunset, December 9th

charcoal thumbprints
smeared
over sheer aquamarine

*

mist in December

late afternoon
just outside Chippewa Falls
the black oaks   the blue silos
the rust-red brick houses
all glazed
pearling in the haze

return of the swans

flocks of swans circling
swirling down with the snow
into the black and rose
clouds of Tell Pond

*

the structure of open water in winter
ten degrees below zero
steam rising out of the rapids
and hanging
fog frozen
crystal over the river

I am having trouble walking
                              against the wind
but the six vultures searching
over the river
simply pivot on it
float   slim black silk
still   kites
sharply tilt   slowly rock
catch
and ride every burst and rush of the thrumming
          foaming wind

*

threnody

the bone-scouring
violins of Shostakovich
the soul weeps
and screams
for Leningrad
the death of Akhmatova

a triptych for May

I
thirteen turkey vultures
fly ballets above the river
silvered
in the cold May wind

II
in the swamped ditches
below the old railroad bed
marsh marigolds
shiver
sun-gold in dew

III
in the shadows between
trillium rise
snow-white
proud   out of the dust
and leaves of the ravines
spilling into the river

el paso de la luz, late November
                    poem as painting

now just after noon
on the western hills
below
in the trees wind-stripped of their leaves
dead leaves spilled over the dust
the bushes   the bent reeds
light ignites
rises and unfurls silver
becomes   scumbled   smeared
twisted   and scratched
whirls glistening silver wires
spins silver loops
sends tendrils of silver
settles still
strokes of hoary smoke

silver richly impastoed
knife-scraped
into glinting shards
slabs and wedges
dug into   smeared with fingers
thumb-gouged   smudged

the thumbprints spiraling outwards
in fine-spun shoots of silver silk
weaving over the grayblack
background   the black branches
caught
forever within
a fine silvery
diamonded sheen
a lattice of silver mist
for the eye

*

how to keep
the windows clean
how to keep the dust off
the mirror

Fall

leaves   auburn
green   gold   gone
forever in hard rain-wind

*

caught in the delight
of the wind stringing
the leaves
silver through the rain

*

have you eaten
of the bitter roots
coughed on salt
are you serious
why do you labor
in these cities
leaving your soul
behind
in the wilderness

I have forgotten to tend
to the things of the hours
soul's balm

*

Jazz I

Coltrane   always
presses each breath
out of his heart
against death

*

query

is coherence necessary
given ecstasies
exploding
out of any instant

Miles Davis playing "It Never Entered My Mind"

how much is at stake in love
souls always at the stake
how difficult to articulate
truth   squelch the grasping self
remorse   agenbite of inwit
for having given pain
again
and again
you need her   like air
like blood
your heart
the song should be
slow   moody   lyrical
pounding

how stupid to have tried
to play a role in this farce
much wiser to wander
off   into the distance
of the long valleys
listen to the winds
find love in those spaces
not scarred by man
or his words
far beyond the cities
that strangle the soul

*

Odrozenie, Poland, 1945

there will not be
another
Renaissance
impossible
after Auschwitz
Kielce
the Black Deaths

enlightenment

at five in the morning
listening to Miles and Coltrane
Robert Johnson and Beethoven
drinking red wine
dancing with you
and the mad Illinois winds

*

beginning

an austere world
the oaks articulate
selves   fine
networks of nerves
synapses   stark black
upthrust
against
thin blue mist

"So What"

God bless   to have been
alive when Miles and Coltrane
gave us those sharp bursts of tenor
and trumpet   call and response
rhythms dancing us out of this
nothingness
towards delight
and the sacred madness of love
a hold on who and what we really are

*

you live most
in brief spaces
jazz   blues   Buson
Monet   Matisse   Monk
the chestnut-sided warbler
bopping down the branch

in Leaf River
far off the roads
we didn't have to
live those other lives
that yellow house
its lights hidden in the shadows of the woods
doors never closed   we danced for days
listening to the blues   Bach   and be bop
talking about Sartre and Camus and Miles
never worried about
living within the machine
did not march off to war   to work

*

for all of this
making you bleed
I must make amends
a day must not be a blur
we let time   and reason
pass   amorphous
take bad photographs
we cannot remember
even the day   at its end

Pierre Bonnard, *Street Scene, Place Clichy*

the thickness of things   their shagginess
the brush strokes that streak across
each inch of the cardboard canvas
the gold scars squiggling in the shop signs
the faces   the costermonger's cart   the walls

gold sprouting   rilling   and sheeting down
beneath the black barrier   the silver-tipped black
furs of the lady parading her poodles
whirling in the foreground
the ways light collides
with stones   wagons   eyes
gold   golden   racing   away

*

under round black hills
misty in the distance
lambs nibbling in the snow

"Blue in Green"

listening to Miles
I smoked Gauloise Disque Bleu
walked down Berkeley streets
dreaming of being Rimbaud

*

after reading Dostoevsky again

those endless silly conversations
even those fueled with beer and wine
rum   tequila
marijuana   mescal
might have gone
somewhere
towards gods   truth
who knows

à la Blake, à la Picasso
        "¡Rimbaud vuelve a casa!"
        Roberto Bolaño

in El Gato
or the 4 Gats of Barcelona
or the Green River bar
we always speak of breaking away
from the Beast
who strangles us
yoking us to the market
we must plod day by day
circling the post
busting the husks
smashing seeds into dust
no time for dreams
no time for love
for breath

August 15

hundreds of hawks
eagles and vultures
tilting   circling   slashing
wind over long hazy Ohio hills
canopies of trees rising higher
up the steep valleys of West Virginia
coming home to the green Shenandoah

*

when you are gone
I am sleepless
without meaning
tormented by the beauty of the rain
the horror of my sins
my failures to speak with you
to square with you
to stand silent in the temple
light spilling through the glass
rose and lavender and silver

these blues will kill you
will drive your soul wild
riff you along
to the outer
edges of your imagination
far past the dusty
skeleton lives we believe
we are living
without love

*

late fall

the afternoon outside
not as black as
the inside   bland
conversations rattling round
exhausted
the only truth   the explosive
cobalt blue of the Cerulean warbler
hopping along the cement
ledge of the window
of the mind

à la René Char

what is the relation
is there an order
of poem to poem
passages
what is order
word to life
not a series
not that joke
"progress"
leaps
jaillisement
the mind
springing
from joy to joy

*

Sunset, 5 PM, January 10th

long magenta shawls
fall across the pale
blue west
the black mazes of trees

waiting for the music
will it be Ravel
Gregorian chants
be bop   Monk
what is
the truth of your blood

*

solo

I remember Coltrane
sweating alone   cold June nights
San Francisco
practicing
between sets
in the alley
next to the Black Hawk
dancing dervish
Pan with a horn
echoing along fog banks
everyone inside drunk
on bourbon   or bliss

Winter Ikon VII

eagles circling
black
across falling
lavender light

*

Ikonostasis

long black and white tailed
red-shouldered hawk sails
cinnamon-breasted
through alleys of oaks
black arcs of branches
ridged with snow

l'étranger

the red-shouldered hawk
rose-breast swelling
over the bone-white
fields and hills
stretched into the distance

*

poem in praise of bebop

there is no thing wilder
more gorgeous   rococo
absurd   than this
essai   to stuff
every second full
avoid the horror
of the vacuum
the brassy legislation
the anarchic lightning of dissonance

after Montale

I do not remember the cathedral
of this our evening   we have forgotten
who has vanished and we do not know
who waits to enter
the narrow doors of the white morning

*

Winter, 1886-1995

this evening the streets
of this simple Wisconsin town seem
just like Paul Signac's *Boulevard de Clichy*
the curves cut through the snow
reds and greens of bricks and moss
rolling round the corner
the black trees frosted
the narrowing
white distance
sailing in

August, after Seferis

gourds
filled with dust
rattling together
angry in the wind

*

Lennie Tristano's *Wow*
like a late March day
Warne Marsh's tenor and Lee
Konitz' alto swirling
together over
Tristano's pointillistic piano
the wild harmony of be-bop
cardinal bobbing
up   and down
through snowmist
blown against blue-bright sky

Nisqually Glacier, Mount Rainier, July 31

a hawk streaks over bowed firs and hemlocks
deer forage in the afternoon shadows
avalanche lilies bob in the wind above the snow
two miles away
across the gorge
we hear the roar and growl and gristling
of rocks cracking and popping downslope
water streaming out of the glacier's snout
ripping out boulders and shattered rocks
falling
gray glacial flour
rivers of stones
stony water
leaping and tumbling and grinding
miles down the mountain

after John Coltrane

I would give you
violets for your furs
cherry-red ribbons for your hair
lambs wool nests for your breasts
the feathers of swans to walk upon
morning and evening winds of jasmine

*

"las otras palabras del viento"

words   save those in poems
do not mean much to me
how to speak truth
when they want to hear
echoes droning in caves

listening to Latin jazz

it's a delight to be alive
to hear the timbales ringing
out into the night when
you don't want to sleep
want to keep dancing
looping with the flutes

*

melancholia
        Chet Baker, *Chan's Song*

lost   hovering
that beautiful sorrow
full   round   midnight
misty   in the skylight
the black trunks of the oaks rising up
that muted trumpet
why does time come back
again
         and again
"how long has this
           been going on"

August harvest

hawks and hummingbirds
magenta heads of Canada thistles
proud stalks of golden woodland sunflowers
and Jerusalem artichokes
towering
over huddled bunches of butter and egg weed
gold yolks spilling out of saffron fronds
pink fountains of surprise lilies
Junior Kimbrough's blue guitar ringing
and clanging   "all night long"
pure white blossoms
riding out of the leathery hedge bindweed
cardinals shooting through
the black-green loops and tangles of grapevines
five sinewy dark-brown mink
bounding down the ditches

snowstorm

on the edge
of the river island
sixteen eagles
flecked and streaked
ghost-white
watching from the tops
of the dark olive willows

*

cool
evening   air after rain
spiced with smoke
and roses
as I pass
raindrops fall
off the heavy magenta
heads of peonies
into the misty grass
this is
more than enough
of a world

About *The Book of Jeweled Visions*

The model for this bundle of poems is the Book of Hours, medieval collections of works of art, celebration, prayers, praise, meditation, and devotion. I have also been guided by the masterful writing of John Knoepfle in his *Poems for the Hours*. I've attempted to set forth the moments when I have been awake to the gracious blessings of beauty and love, the flowers, winds, rains, snows, suns, moons, birds, music, the sounds, art, the colors, all the minute ecstasies I have received. Also, to record some occasional disappointments, failures, weaknesses, and moments of despair.

I continue to add to the larger collection from which I have selected this bundle. Perhaps there will be thousands of jeweled visions.

One does not lay order to the teeming moments, of course. As I wrote in *à la René Char*, this is not a series, it is "leaps/*jaillisement*/the mind/springing/ from joy to joy." I hope you can make these leaps with me, and in your life.